WORLD TRADE CENTER

Tom Greve

Rourke
Educational Media

rourkeeducationalmedia.com

Before Reading:

Building Academic Vocabulary and Background Knowledge

Before reading a book, it is important to tap into what your child or students already know about the topic. This will help them develop their vocabulary, increase their reading comprehension, and make connections across the curriculum.

1. *Look at the cover of the book. What will this book be about?*
2. *What do you already know about the topic?*
3. *Let's study the Table of Contents. What will you learn about in the book's chapters?*
4. *What would you like to learn about this topic? Do you think you might learn about it from this book? Why or why not?*
5. *Use a reading journal to write about your knowledge of this topic. Record what you already know about the topic and what you hope to learn about the topic.*
6. *Read the book.*
7. *In your reading journal, record what you learned about the topic and your response to the book.*
8. *After reading the book complete the activities below.*

Content Area Vocabulary
Read the list. What do these words mean?

commercial
economic
fanaticism
generation
immigrant
influential
internment
Middle East
real estate
seared
suspicion
terrorists
vigilant

After Reading:

Comprehension and Extension Activity

After reading the book, work on the following questions with your child or students in order to check their level of reading comprehension and content mastery.

1. *What is terrorism? (Summarize)*
2. *In what ways do you think this attack changed Americans? (Asking Questions)*
3. *Have you visited Ground Zero or the World Trade Center? Share that experience with us. (Text to self connection)*
4. *What does "If you see something, say something" mean? (Summarize)*
5. *Why were the first two towers referred to as the Twin Towers? (Asking Questions)*

Extension Activity

Ask around! The attacks in New York City happened on September 11, 2001. Most people can recall exactly where they were and what they were doing when they heard of the attacks. Interview your parents, aunts and uncles, grandparents, and teachers about 9/11. Where were they? What do they remember? How has the event changed them?

TABLE OF CONTENTS

People, Places, and Post-War Power 4

Twin Towers 10

9/11 14

If You See Something, Say Something 18

Rising, Remembering 22

Timeline 29

Glossary 30

Index 31

Show What You Know 31

Websites to Visit 31

About the Author 32

Chapter 1

PEOPLE, PLACES, AND POST-WAR POWER

New York City is the biggest and most **influential** city in the United States. The central part of the city is Manhattan.

New York City is home to more than 8 million people. That makes it bigger than Los Angeles and Chicago, the next biggest U.S. cities combined.

New York City

Near the Island's south end sits the World Trade Center (WTC). Just a few city blocks square, the World Trade Center is a symbol of the United States' **economic** power. It is also the central site of the worst day in the country's history.

Rising high above Lower Manhattan, the new World Trade Center dominates the New York City skyline.

The idea to create a World Trade Center began right after the United States's victory in World War II.

By the late 1940s, thanks in part to the U.S. winning the war, New York City grew into the financial and shipping center of the United States and the world.

Powerful People

Perhaps nobody was more responsible for the creation and location of the World Trade Center than the Rockefeller family. John D. Rockefeller, Jr. and his sons owned a lot of Manhattan **real estate**. Right after the war, the Rockefeller family not only worked to bring the newly formed United Nations to New York City, but they helped turn Lower Manhattan into the **commercial** center of the world. They were able to accomplish this through Nelson Rockefeller's position as governor of New York, David Rockefeller's vision for the huge redevelopment project, and the families investments.

Some New Yorkers called the WTC Twin Towers "David and Nelson" after the Rockefeller brothers.

Nelson Rockefeller (1908–1979) was the 48th Governor of New York and the 41st Vice President of the United States.

David Rockefeller (1915–) was the visionary behind the World Trade Center.

By the 1960s a **generation** had passed since the end of World War II. Nelson Rockefeller was now governor of New York State, and construction began on the 16 acre (6.5 hectare) World Trade Center site near the Hudson River in Lower Manhattan.

Construction of the South Tower in 1969.

The construction crew had to create a "bathtub" and build reinforced concrete walls in order to prevent any water from the Hudson River leaking into the building.

Freedom Fact!

Minoru Yamasaki, the architect who designed the World Trade Center, was born to **immigrant** parents from Japan before World War II. During the war, because the U.S. was fighting Japan, many Japanese-Americans had to live in **internment** camps. Yamasaki's family remained free at least partly because of his design skills. Ironically, Yamasaki was afraid of heights.

The design of the World Trade Center called for two of the seven buildings at the site to be identical skyscrapers. Each building was taller than the Empire State Building, which was a few dozen blocks north. It had been the world's tallest building since it opened in 1931.

The mighty Empire State Building was the first building on Earth to soar past 100 stories and was the world's tallest building from 1931 until 1972, when the World Trade Center was finished.

Chapter 2

TWIN TOWERS

When completed in 1972, the World Trade Center, including the 110-floor office Towers, was among the boldest building projects ever done.

Soon after opening, the World Trade Center earned the nickname the Twin Towers because the matching skyscrapers were by far the most eye-popping part of the site.

More than an architectural wonder, the World Trade Center was an exclamation point on America's economic influence around the world and a new trophy on the Manhattan skyline.

The Towers rose very near the Statue of Liberty. Together, they provided two symbols of America's power and promise standing together on the front step of the nation's biggest and busiest city.

Twin Towers By the Numbers:

1,368 feet (417 meters) was the height of the North Tower. That made it 6 feet (1.8 meters) taller than the South Tower.

50,000 people worked in the Twin Towers every day.

43,000 total windows in the Towers to let the sunshine in.

198 miles (319 kilometers) of heating ducts wound through the Towers.

250,000 gallons of paint kept the insides of the Towers looking nice each year.

150,000 people used the subway station below the Towers every day.

One-year-reign as world's tallest buildings. In 1973, Chicago's Sears Tower (now Willis Tower) rose above 1,451 feet (442 meters) to claim the title.

Holy High Wire!

As if their sheer size didn't draw enough attention, in 1974 French tightrope walker Philippe Petit did. He managed to walk back and forth from one Tower to the other on a wire he strung between the two roofs. Thousands of startled, frightened, and delighted people watched from Manhattan's busy streets, nearly a quarter mile below. His stunt made news around the world.

Phillipe Petit (1949–)

Petit's high-wire walk between the two Towers was a feat never accomplished before. It brought recognition to both Petit and the Towers.

Chapter 3

While much of the world saw the Towers as a symbol of American freedom and strength, a group of **terrorists** saw them as a symbol of something else. They wanted revenge for what they thought was too much U.S. power and military involvement in

Freedom Fact!

In 1993, terrorists planted a bomb in the World Trade Center's underground parking garage. The bomb failed to destroy the buildings, but it did kill 6 people, and injured more than a thousand others. The bombing provided a grim clue that terrorists saw the Towers as a target.

the **Middle East**. They planned for years to attack the U.S. and on September 11, 2001, they acted out their terrible plan.

The terrorists knew they would die carrying out their plan, which was to cause as much death and damage as possible. The impact of the planes into the buildings ignited the jets' fuel, causing massive explosions and fires in both Towers.

Nineteen men, all from countries in the Middle East, hijacked four jets and crashed them on purpose. Two planes hit the Twin Towers, another hit the Pentagon in Washington D.C., and a fourth crashed in a Pennsylvania field. It was the deadliest attack on the U.S. in the nation's history.

Firefighters amongst dust and debris after the collapse of the Towers.

Before the day was over, both Towers burned and collapsed. It was a scene so terrifying it changed the world forever. All seven buildings at the World Trade Center site burned or collapsed due to the attack.

The two worst attacks on the U.S. homeland were the Japanese bombing of Pearl Harbor, Hawaii and the terror attacks of September 11, 2001. Both left thousands of Americans dead and changed the course of history. But Pearl Harbor, which thrust the U.S. into World War II, was carried out by an enemy nation's

December 7, 1941, Japanese military attacks U.S. Naval base at Pearl Harbor, Hawaii.

military on a remote naval base. The terrorists of 9/11 were not part of any nation's military. Driven by **fanaticism**, they chose their targets because of their symbolic importance to the United States.

The Port Authority of New York and New Jersey is responsible for all transportation into and out of New York and New Jersey and owns the World Trade Center. The September 11 attack brought all transportation systems to a standstill in and around the city.

Chapter 4

IF YOU SEE SOMETHING, SAY SOMETHING

The World Trade Center disappeared that day. Left in its place was a massive pit of rubble and death. The American people, especially those living in and around New York City, were scared and angry.

Freedom Fact!

*After 9/11, life in the U.S. changed. **Suspicion** became a necessary part of life. People had to show stricter proof of identity and could no longer bring certain items into places like airports, sports stadiums, and large public events. Simple things like backpacks and purses left alone in a public place became a threat.*

The attack prompted the U.S. government to create a Department of Homeland Security to guard against another terrorist attack on U.S. soil.

Since it was individuals, rather than an army, who carried out the attack, regular Americans now have to be **vigilant**. The eyes and ears of the public can help prevent another attack, along with the work of local police, the FBI, and the U.S. military.

Since the attacks, the American public remains on alert. If someone sees something suspicious, they should say something to the police. Then the police can make sure everything is okay.

More than a day after the Towers collapsed, rescue workers still found survivors among the jagged piles of smoking debris. After several days went by without locating any more survivors, the somber task of clearing the World Trade Center site began.

With the nation still in shock and the cleanup process barely underway, U.S. President George W. Bush visited the World Trade Center site that was called "Ground Zero" of the attack. He spoke with firefighters and other workers.

Slowly, workers cleared away twisted steel and debris. By the following summer, the WTC site was clear. What was once the World Trade Center site was again just a vacant construction site.

A ceremony was held on May 30, 2002 marking the end of the cleanup of the WTC site.

Freedom Fact!

The largest steel pieces of the Twin Towers left standing after the attack were shipped back to Pennsylvania where they were originally made to be put on display. Two of the pitchfork-shaped supports remain at the WTC site inside the 9/11 Memorial Museum.

Chapter 5

RISING, REMEMBERING

Shortly after the attack, planning began on a new World Trade Center. In addition to the new buildings, it would include a memorial for all the lives lost on September 11, 2001.

Since 2006 work has advanced higher and higher on the One World Trade Center. The effort to build the new crown jewel of the site is more

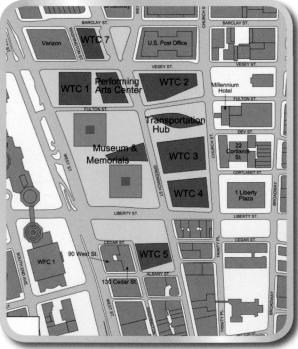

WTC Site Plan

than just a huge construction project. It represents the symbolic healing of a massive physical wound left in New York and the entire country.

November of 2014, One World Trade Center opened for business. The first business to open its doors was Condé Nast, a publishing company.

Freedom Fact!

In May of 2013, One World Trade Center's sleek exterior, made up of 8 interlocking triangular sides, was finished. The building is 1,776 feet (541.3 meters) tall, a height purposely achieved to match the year of the nation's birth and to restore the World Trade Center as home to the nation's tallest building and the tallest building in the Western Hemisphere.

Perhaps more important than the gleaming new skyscraper, the new World Trade Center features the National September 11 Memorial and Museum where the memories of lives lost and bravery in the face of evil are preserved.

The antenna from the Twin Towers is on display at the Memorial and Museum.

In the place where the Twin Towers used to rise are now two sunken Reflecting Pools. The names of all victims of of the attacks, including those who died at the Pentagon and in Pennsylvania, in 2001 and those who died in the WTC attack in 1993 are included on the wall surrounding the pools.

A central struggle in rebuilding the World Trade Center is balancing the effort to bring business back to normal at the site, while showing the proper respect for the national tragedy that unfolded there. Another concern is keeping the site safe from future attacks.

The National September 11 Memorial and Museum is just one of the ways the attack that occurred is commemorated at the World Trade Center.

The Survivor Tree

The last living thing pulled from Ground Zero after 9/11 was a part of a damaged pear tree that workers noticed still grew leaves. They carefully removed the tree and transplanted it in another location to see if it could survive. Low and behold, the mangled bit of tree found sprouting amongst the ruins grew back, and is now back at the World Trade Center, growing new branches and blooming again.

Like the Survivor Tree, the World Trade Center, and the neighborhood surrounding it are coming back to life. Office workers will once again flood the WTC every day, and commerce will hum at the site just like in the days before 9/11.

Osama bin Laden

In May of 2011, the United States military found and killed Osama bin Laden, the lead terrorist believed to have planned and organized the 9/11 attacks. Unfortunately, killing the person most responsible for attacking the World Trade Center has not stopped the threat of terrorism.

Osama bin Laden was found and killed by U.S. Special Forces in a compound in Abottabad, Pakistan.

Osama bin Laden (1957-2011)

The rebuilding of the World Trade Center is happening at the same time as a population boom in the neighborhood surrounding it. A decade after the worst attack in U.S. history tore a gash through Lower Manhattan, people want to live close to the action, in the heart of what is still America's biggest and most influential city.

The new World Trade Center includes a massive Transportation Hub for trains and buses to shuttle people into and out of the WTC and Lower Manhattan in even greater numbers than before 9/11. Its completion is set for 2015.

Today, the World Trade Center rises once again above Lower Manhattan. It remains a symbol of freedom strong enough to heal and rebuild what terrorists knocked down. Soaring and sleek, it offers remembrances of the horrors on 9/11, even as it reaches skyward to meet a brighter future.

TIMELINE

1946 —— New York State government announces its intention to develop a world trade headquarters in New York City.

1951 —— New York City is the unofficial commerce and shipping capital of the world; the United Nations world headquarters opens in Manhattan.

1960 —— Formal plans made, backed by the Rockefeller family, to build complex in Lower Manhattan for world trade.

1964 —— World Trade Center design plans made public. They include twin 110-story office towers.

1968 —— Construction begins.

1973 —— Dedication ceremony officially opens the World Trade Center. Twin Towers recognized as world's tallest buildings.

1993 —— Terrorists detonate a bomb in World Trade Center underground parking garage, killing six people.

Sept. 11, 2001
—— Terrorist attack destroys Twin Towers collapse, more than 2,700 people die at the WTC.

Sept. 12, 2001
—— Last person pulled from the buildings' wreckage alive.

May 2002
—— Crews remove last pieces of ruined buildings from the site.

April 2006
—— After financial and design delays, work begins on the 9/11 Memorial and Museum as well as on One World Trade Center.

May 2011
—— U.S. Special Forces (Navy SEALS) kill Osama bin Laden in Pakistan.

Sept. 11, 2011
—— Ten years to the day after the terrorist attacks, the 9/11 Memorial and Museum opens for families who lost loved ones in the attacks. The next day, it opens to the public.

2014 —— One World Trade Center complete, it is the tallest building in the U.S. Company Conde'Nast, moves in.

GLOSSARY

commercial (kuh-MER-shuhl): having to do with business, or the exchange of goods, services, and money

economic (ehk-uh-NOM-ick): having to do with money and resources

fanaticism (fuh-NAT-uh-sizm): intense, irrational belief or favor in a group or idea

generation (jen-uh-RAY-shuhn): about 20 years, enough time for someone to grow from a child to adult

immigrant (IM-uh-gruhnt): person born in one country, but moves to another to live

influential (in-flew-EHN-shuhl): having the power to affect the way others do things

internment (in-TURN-ment): placing in group detention and isolation

Middle East (Mid-uhl EEST): group of west Asian and north African countries clustered around the eastern end of the Mediterranean Sea

real estate (REEL eh-stayt): land or property including buildings

seared (SEERD): burned, permanently marked

suspicion (suh-SPISH-uhn): questioning or uncertainty regarding someone

terrorists (TAYR-uhr-ists): people who use the threat of unexpected and sudden violence to affect the behavior of others

vigilant (VIJ-eh-luhnt): remaining watchful, on guard

INDEX

Department of Homeland Security   19

Empire State Building   9

Ground Zero   20, 25

Lower Manhattan   5, 8, 27, 28

National September 11 Memorial
and Museum   24, 25

One World Trade Center   22, 23

Petit, Phillippe   13

Port Authority of New York
and New Jersey   17

Reflecting Pools   24

Rockefeller   7, 8

September 11, 2001   14, 16, 17, 22

Survivor Tree   25, 26

terrorists   14, 17, 28

transportation hub   27

United Nations   7

Willis (formerly Sears) Tower   12

World War II   6, 8, 17

Yamasaki, Minoru   8

SHOW WHAT YOU KNOW

1. How many people died at the World Trade Center on 9/11?

2. Before the terrorist attacks on 9/11, what was considered to be the worst tragedy in U.S. history?

3. What type of tree did they find amongst the rubble of the World Trade Center?

4. How tall is One World Trade Center?

5. What are some additions to One World Trade Center to honor the victims lost on 9/11?

WEBSITES TO VISIT

www.panynj.gov/wtcprogress

www.911memorial.org

www.nationalgeographic.com/remembering-9-11

ABOUT THE AUTHOR

Tom Greve is a freelance writer from Chicago. Married with two kids, he's had a lifelong fascination with tall buildings and their symbolic power. He has visited Ground Zero in New York City and looks forward to visiting the new World Trade Center.

Meet The Author!
www.meetREMauthors.com

PHOTO CREDITS: Cover © Felix Lipov; Title Page, page 5 © Leonard Zhukovsky; Page Topper ©Songquan Deng; page 4 © Cesar Barba; page 6, 15, 17 © Library of Congress; page 7 © Visions of America, White House, Diane Bondareff/AP Images; page 8 © usrlman; page 9 © Markus Gann; page 10 © bluebird13; page 11 © lbrink mmx; page 13 © Alan Welner/AP Images; page 15 Dan Howell; page16 © Larry Bruce; page 17 © Jim Collins/AP Images; page 19 © wellesenterprises; page 20 © Doug Mills/AP Images; page 21 © Jeffrey M. Frank, Shawn Baldwin/AP Images; page 22 © Mangoman88; page 23 © Alexpro9500, Ritu Jethani; page 24 © Cpenler, John Anderson Photo; page 25 © Alex9500, Christopher Penler; page 26 © Anonymous/AP Images; page 27 © leungphotography

Edited by: Luana Mitten
Cover and interior design by: Renee Brady

Library of Congress PCN Data

World Trade Center / Tom Greve
(Symbols of Freedom)
ISBN 978-1-63430-042-1 (hard cover)
ISBN 978-1-63430-072-8 (soft cover)
ISBN 978-1-63430-101-5 (e-Book)
Library of Congress Control Number: 2014953357

Also Available as:

ROURKE'S

e-Books

Printed in the United States of America, North Mankato, Minnesota